VOLUME I

Stories and Illustrations by Gail Delger

Copyright © Gail Delger 2016

GailDelger.com

BirdDo.com

This book is dedicated to all my family and friends who have supported my art career. Tim, Nicole and Kevin for being my best critiquers. To all of my friends who have encouraged me to get a book together and finally to my husband Al for his many years of support for my art.

Larry looks up his family tree...literally. He sees that he has quite a variety of relatives. Some good, some not so good. Luckily they only have to get together once a year for the holiday, and that of course is Arbor Day.

Three birds fly up to find out why Lenny the goat is on the roof. Lenny tells them that he climbed up there to see if he could fly. They giggled and snorted (as much as a bird can) and then told him that he better flap his ears as fast as he can, because they think he is headed for a hard landing.

Alice stands on the dog bowl so Spike will know who's the boss. She says. "If you want food, you need to sit and speak." Spike thinks. "A skinny-legged bird is not going to tell me what to do. Maybe I'll just walk by and lift my leg."

The dogs and their friend, Burt the bird, look for the pesky neighborhood cat. Burt says, "I don't see her, but let's keep watch for a little while. She's sneaky and she thinks she can outsmart us. We'll show her!"

Dirk stops by his friend Mark's house to help with a stuck cat. Mark said it rained cats and dogs yesterday, and a cat got caught in the tree. "REALLY!" Dirk said. "It didn't even rain at my house."

Betty and Marilyn take their kids to work. They are two of the rare 4-legged birds that work at the circus sideshow. They show their kids that being different has its rewards. One time they were on Ewe Tube (the sheep channel), and from that, people recognized them on the streets and wanted to take selfies with them.

Heading into town, the Warbler family comes to a speed bump,
aka Mr. Turtle. They like the hill, it makes the walk more interesting.
Luckily it's not raining—that shell can be as slippery as...well, you know.

Marian rides her dog, Duke, to the mall for the dog show. Their category is "dogs you can ride." The security guard outside says, "No horses allowed." Marian tries to explain that Duke is her dog. Duke barks...then the guard lets them pass.

The birds do their wing walking on the weekends. Three of them are getting pretty good. Then there is Rita who loses her balance and Roger who is very lazy today. Roger may be standing in line at the unemployment tree soon.

The record for the highest pogo stick bounce is this guy. Wilfred the bird, coming to your neighborhood any day now.

Martha is teaching her kids how to fly. They are not flying over fast food restaurants like they had hoped. Looks like farm fresh, sorry—no french fries today.

The Warbler family goes out looking for a new house. They are overwhelmed with all of the choices. Of course the kids want the one with the pool. and Mrs. Warbler wants an open floor plan. Mr. Warbler just wants to quit shopping and go home.

These two siblings don't even see their mom dropping the worm, because they are watching the UFOs. Their mom doesn't like it when they get distracted. They say, "Mom, look, look behind you." She's not going to fall for that again. Last time when they told her to look, she turned her back on them, and they snuck into the cookie jar, I mean, worm jar.

Walking with his daughter and grandson makes Elrod see the family resemblance. Besides having similar tail feathers, they all have the same bird walk. You know, two steps—chirp, one step—whistle.

Harry, Joe and Shirley carpool every day. They have always taken the water route. Someday they will hear the phrase, "as the crow flies," and a light bulb will go off.

Marvin takes his kids fishing. The fish are aware of the birds, but they don't panic. Their mom says, "These are Dodo birds, and they are not very good at fishing." And you thought Dodo birds couldn't fly!

George meets his kids at the bus stop. He tells them to take their boots off when they get home, because wet footprints in the house drives their mom crazy.

The birds get the crowd to start cheering for the home team. Jenny, on the top of the pyramid, gets ready to do a flip and notices that her spotter is taking a break. The crowd tries to egg her on—Please don't egg a bird on, that's cruel.

Hugh, Dew and Lou like to drive their go karts on the weekend. Vroooom! Vroooom! That sound is from the go-karts, not the birds. You try to make that sound with a beak. It can't be done.

Marie, Glen and Junior slide down the hill near their home. They have trouble finding winter wear for birds, so their feet and legs get very cold. Of course they could fly south and they wouldn't have this problem...unless there is a Polar Vortex.

His name is Bloop. Before he was born, his mom and dad were tidying up around the nest. When he started to hatch, his dad said, "What was that sound?" His mom said, "I don't know, it sounded like...'bloop'." The rest is history. Oh, I forgot to mention, their last name is Dee-Doop.

Back from giving a tour of the harbor, Priscilla stops at the dock to let the tourists off. The Coast Guard heads out to make their rounds. They tell her that she is carrying too much weight. She thinks..."Surely they are talking about my passenger load."

Shhhhh...Bud is about to putt. If he makes this one, he will win the tournament and go down in history as the bird with the lowest score since the great Tiger Woodpecker.

The husband and wife piggy-back race is always exciting. The fans cheer them across the finish line. Two of them will win, which doesn't seem right. Two winners in the final four—that's unheard of.

Shopping with the kids can be fun and a little stressful. Peggy remembers the good old days when her husband would bring home worms for everyone, and there was no need to go to the store. Now, one of her kids is allergic to peanuts and the other is lactose-intolerant, and we all know both are found in worms.

Thomas takes his kids out for lunch. They look over the menu before going in. He says. "We are not eating anything that has two legs today." "How will we know how many legs it has before we order it?" the kids ask. "Don't they teach you that at school?" he asks. "No. Dad. we are learning our haze. bees and seas right now. You know...all about weather. insects and water."

The flock plays hopscotch in the alley every day. The other flocks have painted the walls with graffiti. Those graffiti artists sure know what's trending now. BirdDo does rule!

Wait wait wait! You two slow down and go smell those roses. then be on your way.

Willard the rat, runs through the house on his way to a family reunion next door. Oh no, he forgot that he is supposed to bring the cheese. He'll send two of his cousins back to get the cheese. The second mouse always gets the cheese, you know.

Eddie watches the cookies bake and stays a safe distance away so that he doesn't burn his beak. His mom says a cookie a day keeps the doctor away...I don't know if it's true, but it sure sounds good.

Living in a telephone pole has its good and bad points. The ability to see long distances is good, but that constant phone ringing can drive a bird crazy.

Nelson is a scientist. Growing up he heard people say, "Nelson's not a rocket scientist." He wanted to prove them wrong, so he went to school and got a degree from the Bird Institute of Technology. Now he is a Rocket Scientist...really, he is!!

The three finalists anxiously await the judge's decision. The winner may seem obvious, but they are judged by beak to body ratio. They are all hoping that their beaks don't make their tail feathers look big.

Pamela gets her teeth cleaned. The dentist tells her she needs to quit eating berries. They are staining her teeth. Pamela tells the dentist that she loves berries. He tells her to try the new "berry-free diet." All of Alfred Hitchcock's birds are on it, and it's trending on the internet too!

Elwood is late for work. His kids catch the tail wind to school.
Watch out...your dad ate beans last night!

Jerry got caught in the hallway without a pass. Principal Grouse tells him and his little friend Judi that they must go to detention today. As they walk away, they both burst out laughing. Mr. Grouse's fly was down.

Birds are drawn to Gilbert...literally. His magnetism prevents him from having a day to himself. For some reason when the sun goes down, the force of the magnetic pull decreases, and the birds are able to drop off and fly home. If you see Gilbert, be sure to turn off all of your electronic devices.

Have you ever wondered if you could lift four of your friends over your head all at once? Marty wanted to see if he could and realized that his fat muscular legs were just the ticket. Please don't try this at home. Marty has been training for years.

Once thought to be extinct the Man-Head Bird walks the streets in the suburbs. The birds tweet about the MHB, telling everyone to watch out. He is harmless, but a little top-heavy. If he leans forward too far, he tips over, and those two could be goners. Run, little birds, run!

Walking around on tree branches can really do a number on a bird's nails. Lucille has been giving pedicures for nine years. She remembers one time when a bird came in with five toes on each foot. Boy, was that ever a nightmare!

When the carnival comes to town, the birds all flock to ride the Ferris wheel. They've watched people stand in line for the ride and wanted to know what all the excitement was about. After going around a couple of times, they decide that they will stick with the thermal updrafts near the low-pressure systems. They are more fun...and little or no waiting.

Jethro walks his bird Claude to the circus for a day of work. The bird does some amazing things. First, he can lay golden eggs. Just the idea that he can lay eggs is amazing! I can't tell you anything else, because you really need to pay to see the show.

First day on the job, the boss teaches the new employees about stocking the shelves. They think they have job security because it takes all three of them to reach the top shelf. There aren't any security cameras, but they sense that they are being watched.

How many birds does it take to change a light bulb? Looks like three, but why are they changing a light bulb that is perfectly good?

Okay, you three need to make sure no one touches these masterpieces. Remember, if they get too close, go peck them on the shoulder...several times if needed.

Dudley is taking his kids to the parade today. The stilts get them up high enough to see over the crowd. Now they don't have to watch from the power lines where they have those stupid spacing rules.

Uncle Ralph is taking his nieces out to the movies. They are going to see the Alfred Hitchcock thriller about a large group of people who terrorize a small town of birds. Wait...what?

Gail Delger has been painting professionally since 1990. She is a multi-media artist who enjoys creating 2D and 3D art. Whimsical subjects appear in many of her paintings.